AMAZING ANIMAL Q&As

Why Don't Fish Have Eyelashes?

by Nancy Dickmann

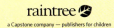 raintree

a Capstone company — publishers for children

Raintree is an imprint of Capstone Global Library Limited, a company incorporated in England and Wales having its registered office at 264 Banbury Road, Oxford, OX2 7DY – Registered company number: 6695582

www.raintree.co.uk
myorders@raintree.co.uk

Edited by Megan Peterson
Designed by Ted Williams
Original illustrations © Capstone Global Library Limited 2022
Picture research by Jo Miller
Production by Spencer Rosio
Originated by Capstone Global Library Ltd
Printed and bound in India

978 1 3982 1564 1 (hardback)
978 1 3982 1572 6 (paperback)

British Library Cataloguing in Publication Data
A full catalogue record for this book is available from the British Library.

Acknowledgements
We would like to thank the following for permission to reproduce photographs: BluePlanetArchive.com: Dan Burton, 10, Jeff Rotman, 11; Science Source: Danté Fenolio, 19; Shutterstock: Deyan Georgiev, 8, Diego Cervo, 6, gallimaufry, 14, KPG_Payless, Cover, lfdf, 20, Noheaphotos, 7, owatta, design element, Red orange, 20–21, satit_srihin, 5, Tom Goaz, 13, Vlad61, 17, Wiratchai wansamngam, 9, ZenStockers, design element; SuperStock: Norbert Wu, 15

Every effort has been made to contact copyright holders of material reproduced in this book. Any omissions will be rectified in subsequent printings if notice is given to the publisher.

Contents

Words in **bold** are in the glossary.

Look, mum, no lashes!

Have you ever had a pet fish? You don't look much like a fish. But you do have some things in common. Fish have a **backbone**, just like you do. They have a mouth. They have two eyes. But their eyes are not quite the same as yours. A fish has no eyelashes!

What eyelashes do

Eyelashes do an important job. Dust in the air can bother eyes. Eyelashes **protect** our eyes. They catch dust. They also **sense** objects coming close. This tells us we need to close our eyes.

Fish live underwater. They don't have to worry about dust. So they don't need eyelashes! Most fish are missing another body part too. Can you guess what it is?

Spot what's missing

Where are your eyelashes? On your eyelids, of course! When you blink, the eyelids close over your eyes. This helps clear away dust. It also keeps your eyes wet. Dry eyes can hurt.

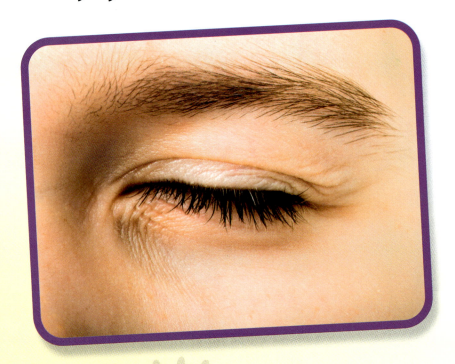

Most fish don't have eyelids. Their eyes are always wet. They won't dry out underwater. This means that most fish can't close their eyes.

Scary sharks

Sharks are fish. They don't have eyelashes. But they do have eyelids! The lids protect their eyes. But a shark's eyelids can't close all the way.

Sharks attack **prey**. Sometimes the prey fights back! It might poke the shark's eyes. Some sharks also have a third eyelid. This clear lid slides over the eye to protect it.

Do fish sleep?

A fish can't close its eyes. But it still needs to sleep. When fish rest, they slow down. They often sink lower in the water.

Some fish keep moving to breathe. Water must move through their **gills** at all times. These fish keep swimming even when they're asleep!

The world's weirdest eyes

Fish don't have eyelashes. But some fish have weird eyes! "Four-eyed fish" really have two eyes. Each eye is split into two parts. One part looks above the water. The other looks below.

A barreleye fish lives deep underwater. Its eyes are inside its head. The head is see-through! The eyes see right through the skin. They **swivel** upwards to see prey.

What do fish see?

Most fish need to see. Seeing helps them find food. It also helps them look out for danger. Fish can see movement. Some fish can see colour.

Many fish use other senses to find food. Some fish, such as sharks, have a good sense of smell. Many fish feel **vibrations** in the water. This tells them where other creatures are.

The midnight zone

The deep ocean is called the midnight zone. It is very dark. Light from the sun doesn't reach it. Glowing sea creatures make the only light.

Some deep-sea fish can't see at all. Others have huge eyes. Some are shaped like **telescopes**. They collect tiny amounts of light. But none of these fish have eyelashes!

19

Design a fish

What you need:

- paper
- coloured pencils or felt-tip pens

What to do:

1. Most fish have some body parts in common. Look at some pictures of fish to see what they are. Can you see gills and eyes? Can you see a mouth and fins?

2. Think about what your fish will be like. Will it be a fast swimmer? Will it hunt prey? Will it live deep underwater?

3. Decide what body parts your fish will need.

4. Draw your fish and colour it. Label the body parts. Give your fish a fun name!

Glossary

backbone set of connected bones that run down the middle of the back; the backbone is also called the spine

gill body part on the side of a fish; fish use their gills to breathe

prey animal that is hunted by another animal for food

protect keep safe

sense way of knowing about your surroundings; sight, smell, hearing, taste and touch are senses

swivel turn or rotate around a central point

telescope tool people use to look at objects that are far away

vibration fast movement back and forth

Find out more

Books

Fish (Animal Classification), Angela Royston (Raintree, 2016)

How Do Dolphins Sleep? (Crazy Animal Facts), Nancy Furstinger (Raintree, 2020)

Shark: Killer King of the Ocean (Top of the Food Chain), Angela Royston (Raintree, 2020)

Websites

www.bbc.co.uk/bitesize/topics/z6882hv
Learn more about animals, from mammals to minibeasts.

www.dkfindout.com/uk/animals-and-nature/animal-kingdom
Find out more about the animal kingdom.

Index